Ladybird Readers

There Are Ten

Notes to teachers, parents, and carers

The **Ladybird Readers** Beginner level helps young language learners to become familiar with key conversational phrases in English. The language introduced has clear real-life applications, giving children the tools to hold their first conversations in English.

This book focuses on counting from one to ten, and provides practice of using the phrases "there is" and "there are", as well as animal names in English.

There are some activities to do in this book. They will help children practice these skills:

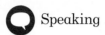 Speaking    Listening*    Reading

*To complete these activities, listen to the audio downloads available at **www.ladybirdeducation.co.uk**

Series Editor: Sorrel Pitts
Chants by Sorrel Pitts

LADYBIRD BOOKS

UK | USA | Canada | Ireland | Australia
India | New Zealand | South Africa

Ladybird Books is part of the Penguin Random House group of companies
whose addresses can be found at global.penguinrandomhouse.com.
www.penguin.co.uk   www.puffin.co.uk   www.ladybird.co.uk

Penguin
Random House
UK

Text inspired by *1, 2, 3 to the Zoo* by Eric Carle, first published in Great Britain by Hamish Hamilton, 1969
This version first published by Ladybird Books 2024
001

Text and illustrations copyright © Penguin Random House LLC, 1968, 1987
Adapted text and artwork copyright © 2024 by Penguin Random House LLC
The moral right of the original author/illustrator has been asserted

Printed in China

The authorized representative in the EEA is Penguin Random House Ireland, Morrison Chambers, 32 Nassau Street, Dublin D02 YH68

A CIP catalogue record for this book is available from the British Library

ISBN: 978-0-241-58760-7

All correspondence to:
Ladybird Books
Penguin Random House Children's
One Embassy Gardens, 8 Viaduct Gardens, London SW11 7BW

MIX
Paper | Supporting
responsible forestry
FSC® C018179

There Are Ten

Inspired by
1, 2, 3 to the Zoo
by Eric Carle

There is one elephant.

There are two hippos.

There are three giraffes . . . 3

and there are four lions.

There are five bears.

There are six crocodiles.

There are seven seals . . .

and there are
eight monkeys.

There are nine snakes.

There are ten birds!

Your turn!

1   **Talk with a friend.**

How many giraffes?

Three!

How many birds?

Ten!

2 Listen. Color in the words.

1

| bear | lion |

2

| seven | seal |

3

| hippo | monkey |

4

| five | nine |

3 Read and clap!

There is one elephant. There are two hippos.
There are three giraffes. There are four lions.
Four lions, hooray!

There are five bears. There are six crocodiles.
There are seven seals. There are eight monkeys.
Eight monkeys, hooray!

There are nine snakes. There are ten birds.
Ten birds, hooray!